Cyber Education Literature Series

Copyright © 2020 Air Force Association

CyberPatriot – the National Youth Cyber Education Program – was created by the Air Force Association (AFA) to inspire K–12 students toward careers in cybersecurity or other science, technology, engineering, and mathematics (STEM) disciplines critical to our nation's future.

More information about the CyberPatriot program can be found at: www.uscyberpatriot.org

ISBN: 978-1-09830-104-0

BEN THE CYBER DEFENDER

Ben loves every little thing about computers. He is always safe online, and he is always trying to learn more.

"Yes! Network secured!" exclaimed Ben.

He also prevented his grandfather from getting scammed by a phishing email.

"Ben, can you help me verify my bank account?" Grandpa asked. "I am not sure how it's done."

Ben looked closely at the email. "Oh no, Grandpa! Don't click on that link. Look closely—that's a fake email address and the message is full of typos. This is a phishing email. Delete it immediately and I will help you report it to your bank."

From: postmaster150@emailmaker.co.au
Sent: Friday, June 8, 2019 4:28 PM
To: <gpa@email.com>
Subject:

Dear Customer,
Sorry for a inconvenience. We are face some technical difficulty with your account right away and so you cannot access your account. Please click on the link below to verify your account and unlock.
Access your Account

He saved his neighbor, Emma, from falling prey to a cybercriminal who was chatting with her online, pretending to be her friend and inviting her to parties.

"Hey Ben! I am going to a party with my new friend, Amanda! I am very excited to meet her and all her friends," said Emma.

"Hmm... no profile photo, no mutual friends, and no posts. Emma, don't go. This is obviously a fake profile."

Emma was scared. "A fake profile? Now that you mention it, when I asked Amanda about her profile photo, she said she is too shy. But, not having any posts or photos is very suspicious indeed. Thanks for warning me, Ben."

"You are welcome, Emma. You should probably block this 'Amanda' person and warn all your friends about her," Ben suggested.

One day, Ben was hanging out with his cousin, Ethan, at his Aunt Amy's house.

Ethan loved to use social media. He had accounts on all the latest apps! He would "check-in" on CyberPal whenever he went somewhere new. He posted daily updates about where he was hanging out, who he was with, and what he had planned for the day. He was constantly posting online about every tiny detail of his life.

Hangry HotDogs
456 S. Michael St.

HOME SWEET HOME

CyberPal
photogram

My pal Mickey loves
to play in the park!!

Ben was worried about Ethan's addiction to social media and he had a bad feeling that Ethan would soon find himself in trouble due to his reckless online behavior.

Little did Ben know that trouble had already arrived.

Aunt Amy came into the room with her phone in her hand, looking questioningly at Ethan.

"Ethan, what is this message you sent on CyberPal? Which vacation are you talking about?"

Ethan was confused. "What message? I didn't send you any messages on CyberPal."

Ethan's phone started going off. "Hold on! I'm getting texts from my friends saying the same thing. They all apparently received a message from me about a vacation." He showed his phone to Ben in a panic.

"Calm down, Ethan," Ben said. "I think I know what's going on. Your account was hacked and whoever hacked it sent that message to all your friends. The message is actually malware. Anyone who clicks on the link is redirected to a page with flashing ads and warning signs and this triggers the download of a virus. Because of all the pop-ups, it's too hard to stop the download. If they have anti-malware installed on their devices, they might be safe. If they don't have it installed, they won't be so lucky."

Ethan couldn't believe it. "Hacked? How is that possible? Why would anyone hack my account?"

"There's no particular reason. Just like people do bad things in real life, there are cybercriminals waiting to prey on unsuspecting victims online," Ben said. "You might not realize it, but your personal data is very valuable to many people. You should guard your personal information like you would guard any of your precious possessions."

"But my CyberPal account is password protected and only I know my password. It's the name of my pet dog, Mickey," said Ethan.

"The same dog you post about day and night?" Ben shook his head. "Ethan, that's a terrible password! You should never use personal information as a password."

"Let me go warn your dad before he clicks on the link, too," said Aunt Amy as she dashed out of the room.

"Ben, you should call your mom. I bet she can help us," Ethan said, with a hopeful look on his face.

Ben looked determined as he sat down at the computer. "My mom is traveling for work today, but don't worry. I can help."

He knew exactly what to do. "I think the hacker must be someone who has some way of getting information on you. Since you have so many friends on CyberPal and your account is public, it could be anyone."

CyberPal

Report Account Hacked

Please click the "My Account is Hacked" button if you believe that someone has hacked into your account or if you suspect any suspicious activity involving your account.

[My Account is Hacked]   [Cancel]

"We need to first report that your account was hacked."

Ben navigated through the CyberPal security settings like a pro, reporting the hack and changing Ethan's account to private.

"Ok, Ethan. The next step is to change your password. You should use at least 10 characters with a combination of upper-case and lower-case letters, numbers, and symbols," Ben explained.

"Remember, never share your password with anyone and never use the same password for all your accounts!"

Ethan understood now why strong passwords were important, but knew the problem wasn't solved quite yet. "But what about my friends who clicked on the link? How can we help them?"

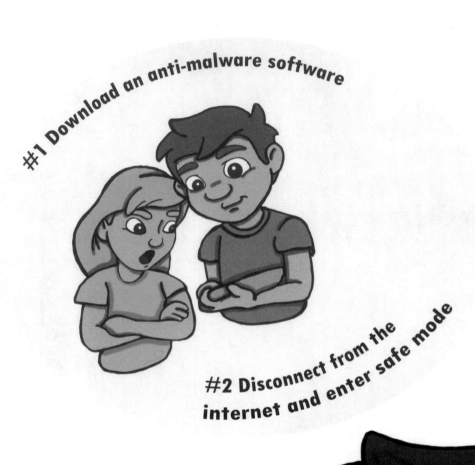

#1 Download an anti-malware software

#2 Disconnect from the internet and enter safe mode

#3 Run a threat scan to detect the virus

#4 Get rid of the infected files and restart device

"We need to contact them immediately. We don't have much time to waste. If this virus keeps spreading, the whole town might be affected."

Ben thrived under the pressure, embarking on the most exciting adventure of his life. He was meant to be a cyber defender. After just a few hours, Ben was able to walk everyone through the virus removal process and save the whole town from the brink of technological disaster.

The next day, the whole town was abuzz with news of how Ben saved them from an impending cyber crisis.

His exploits even made the local newspaper!

"Here you go Ben, a brand-new computer!" the Mayor said smiling down at Ben. "The whole town wants you to keep learning about cybersecurity and making us proud!"

Ben's exciting adventures even caught the attention of the CyberSquad—a team of cyber heroes who fight cybercrime and protect vulnerable computer users from cyberattacks!

In fact, Ben was just the type of squad member they were looking for.

The next day at Ben's house...

"Ben, we are really impressed by you. We need someone just like you to be a part of the CyberSquad team. Will you join us?" asked Sarah the Cyber Hero.

"Ben, what happened?" asked mom. She could hear him all the way in the kitchen.

"Mom! I can't wait to grow up and become a cybersecurity expert like you. I will help anyone who is in cyber danger!" Ben said excitedly.

Ben's mom beamed at him. "You are already helping so many people," she said. "I am really proud of you." Ben's mom was right. The more he learned about cybersecurity, the more he made it his mission to help his friends and family whenever they found themselves in cyber danger.

There was that one time when Ben helped his Uncle Mike, who could have fallen victim to identity theft when using an open Wi-Fi connection to buy a shirt.

"Don't use your credit card over the open network, Uncle Mike! Many people get their identities stolen when using public Wi-Fi to send personal information," Ben said.

Uncle Mike looked shocked. "Thanks for warning me Ben. I was just about to use my credit card to buy a new shirt."

FREE Wi-fi

Ca

"Yes! It would be an honor," replied Ben enthusiastically.

And just like that, Ben became the newest member of the CyberSquad. His first mission: attend an AFA CyberCamp at his school.

ABOUT THE AUTHOR | Madhu has always enjoyed writing and loved this opportunity to write a children's book that is not only fun to read, but also educational.

She has worked with youth-focused nonprofits in Germany, Austria, India, and the United States. She joined the CyberPatriot team in 2018 and really appreciates the chance to work with children while also learning about cybersecurity.

MADHU DEBNATH

ABOUT THE ILLUSTRATOR | Michael first became fascinated by illustration and animation after seeing Ursula the Sea Witch in *The Little Mermaid* (1989).

He has done work for businesses, private clients and authors. He even lived out his dream for several years as an artist at Walt Disney World.

Michael also did the illustrations for *Sarah the Cyber Hero*, the first book in the Cyber Education Literature Series.

MICHAEL D. RAU